The Leo Frank Case: The Controversial History of the Arrest and Trial of a Jewish Man Wrongly Convicted of Murder in the Early 20th Century

By Charles River Editors

A picture taken during the raids

About Charles River Editors

Charles River Editors is a boutique digital publishing company, specializing in bringing history back to life with educational and engaging books on a wide range of topics. Keep up to date with our new and free offerings with this 5 second sign up on our weekly mailing list, and visit Our Kindle Author Page to see other recently published Kindle titles.

We make these books for you and always want to know our readers' opinions, so we encourage you to leave reviews and look forward to publishing new and exciting titles each week.

Introduction

"The pathological conditions in the city menaced the home, the state, the schools, the churches, and, in the words of a contemporary Southern sociologist, the 'wholesome industrial life.' The institutions of the city were obviously unfit to handle urban problems. Against this background, the murder of a young girl in 1913 triggered a violent reaction of mass aggression, hysteria, and prejudice." - Leonard Dinnerstein, historian

The Jim Crow South has been notorious for miscarriages of justice for decades, and cases like the Scottsboro Boys continue to be commemorated for the manner in which institutionalized racism ensured the wrongful convictions of minorities. The attention given to these cases raised nearly every potential issue implicating criminal procedure among the states. While the Bill of Rights had ensured a number of rights for criminal defendants, the states had previously been allowed to interpret those rights, leading to instances where defendants weren't provided adequate legal representation. For example, the case of the Scottsboro Boys compelled the U.S. Supreme Court to order new trials in *Powell v. Arizona* (1932), which went a long way to determining and codifying some of the rights of criminal defendants in state courts.

However, blacks weren't the only ones discriminated against in the South, as the Leo Frank case made clear in the 1910s. While 20th century anti-Semitism has been (and often continues to be) viewed mainly as a problem in European countries like France and Germany, anti-Semitic hysteria led to one of the most shocking episodes of mob justice in early 20th century America.

In 1913, Mary Phagan, a young Georgia factory girl and the daughter of tenant farmers, was raped and killed, and suspicion fell upon Leo Frank, the Jewish-American factory manager, who was subsequently arrested, tried, and convicted of her murder based on the thinnest of circumstantial evidence. The entire case against Frank rested on the testimony of the factory janitor, Jim Conley, despite the fact Conley had been arrested almost immediately after Frank when he was spotted washing what appeared to be blood off his clothes. Subsequent investigations determined that Conley had written notes found by Phagan's body, and Conley's testimony explained this extremely incriminating evidence away by claiming Frank had dictated the notes to him to write down before they moved the body to the location it was discovered. Modern historians now believe Conley committed the murder himself, but based on his testimony, Conley only received a sentence of one year for being an accomplice after the fact.

The conviction was controversial enough in its day that Georgia Governor John M. Slaton commuted Frank's death sentence, which stirred up such a frenzy that a mob driven by their prejudices took what they saw as justice into their own hands. The result was a stark reminder of the roles that race, class, and religion played in the South during the beginning of the 20th century.

The Leo Frank Case: The Controversial History of the Arrest and Trial of a Jewish Man Wrongly Convicted of Murder in the Early 20th Century examines the events that led up to the trial, how it was conducted, and the horrible aftermath. Along with pictures depicting important people, places, and events, you will learn about Leo Frank like never before.

The Leo Frank Case: The Controversial History of the Arrest and Trial of a Jewish Man Wrongly Convicted of Murder in the Early 20th Century

Crossing Paths

Leo Max Frank was born on April 17, 1884, in Cuero, Texas, the son of Rudolph Frank and Rachel Jacobs Frank. Rudolph Frank was of German ancestry, born in Dusseldorf in November 1844 before emigrating from Germany to the United States around 1869. He settled in Brooklyn, where he met and married Rachel, then 22, in 1881.

Shortly after their marriage, Rudolph and Ruth moved to Texas, settling in the small ranching town of Cuero, where among other activities Rudolph served as the local postmaster. However, when Leo was just three months old, the family moved back to Brooklyn, and Leo attended public schools and graduated from the Pratt Institute in 1902. It was noted in the July 1902 *Pratt Institute Monthly* that he excelled on the school debate team, and his course work and stellar grades earned him admission to Cornell University.

At Cornell, which he attended from 1902 until his graduation in 1906, he majored in mechanical engineering. He also participated in extracurricular activities such as photography and chess, as well as playing basketball and tennis on the college teams. As he had at Pratt, he was a member of the Henry Morse Stephens debate team from 1902-1906, eventually becoming a debating coach for the Cornell Congress of 1906. The Cornell Senior Class Book in 1906 listed Frank as a member of the Cornell Society of Mechanical Engineering, and its entry for Frank said in the humorous tone typical of the time, "Leo Max Frank hails from sleepy Brooklyn, famed for graveyards, breweries and baby carriages. Blossoming in the cotton fields of Texas and finding southern life too easy, he migrated to New York's slumberland. The far-famed beauty of Ithaca's scenery induced him to choose Cornell as his Alma Mater. His genius found expression in three-phased generators and foundry work, where he soon gained the reputation of being the champion hot-air artist of the University by his happy faculty of talking all day and saying nothing. His services as a debating coach for the Congress debate teams have made him a fame hard to equal. This proficiency as an air shooter will doubtless win Max success as a gas jet."

Leo and his family

After his graduation, Frank took a summer position as a draftsman for the B. F. Sturtevant Company in Hyde Park, Massachusetts. He returned to Brooklyn in the fall, where in 1907 he took a job as a testing engineer and draftsman for the National Meter Company.

It was at this time that Frank received an invitation from his uncle, Moses Frank, who lived in Atlanta. Moses had moved to the United States from Düdelsheim in Hesse-Darmstadt in 1856 and had eventually settled in Atlanta, where he became a naturalized American citizen in 1865 after the end of the Civil War. He made his fortune speculating in cotton and cotton oil, investing in numerous business ventures both in Atlanta and in New York City. In 1907, Moses Frank and paper manufacturing magnate Sigmund Montag had partnered in the National Pencil Company, a factory based in Atlanta.

After that company was started, Moses offered his nephew the opportunity to travel to Atlanta to meet with him and the other investors about a position in the company. In late October 1907, Frank traveled to Atlanta for the meeting, and he was quickly offered a management position which he readily accepted.

Given that he knew nothing about the manufacture of pencils, it was first necessary for Frank to fill this gap in his knowledge, so after a short time in New York City, Frank traveled in November 1907 to Germany, where in December he began a nine month apprenticeship to study pencil manufacturing at the Eberhard Faber pencil factory. Faber had been manufacturing pencils in the United States since 1861, with a factory in Brooklyn since 1874.

Once his apprenticeship was completed, Frank returned to the United States on August 1, 1908. Leaving Brooklyn on August 4, he arrived by train in Atlanta on August 6 and began work as superintendent of the factory on August 10.

While Leo Frank was completing his education, maturing into adulthood, and beginning his career in Atlanta, the young girl whose tragic death would change his life forever was growing up nearby. Mary Phagan was born on Jun 1, 1899 into a family of tenant farmers. Her father died shortly before she was born, so after her birth, her mother, Francis Phagan, moved the family back to her hometown of Marietta, Georgia. When Mary was seven, Francis moved the family again, this time to East Point, just south of Atlanta, and opened a boarding house. In 1909, when Mary was 10, she left school to go to work part-time at a textile mill. Francis Phagan married John William Coleman in 1912, and the family moved into Atlanta. It was there, in 1913 at the age of 13, that Mary took a job at the National Pencil Company.

Mary Phagan

Frank settled into his job as factory superintendent at a salary of $180 per month with a portion of the factory's profits, and shortly after his arrival in Atlanta, he met Lucille Selig. Selig was an Atlanta native, born in 1888 as one of three daughters to Emil Selig and Josephine Cohen. Her family was prominent in Atlanta's Jewish community, the largest in the South. Lucille's maternal grandfather, Levi Cohen, had been part of founding the first synagogue in Atlanta, and the family was active in Atlanta's Jewish social life, engaging in philanthropic work and supporting the Reformed Synagogue. Emil Selig worked as a salesman for the West Disinfecting Company, a firm that manufactured soaps and industrial cleaning supplies.

Lucille's formal education ended with her graduation from high school in 1906, but she was considered clever, witty, and well-read. After Leo and Lucille met in August of 1908, he began to seriously court the young lady, and they became engaged in 1910. The *Atlanta Journal* announced the wedding: "The wedding of Miss Lucile Selig and Mr. Leo Frank was a pretty event which took place last evening at the home of the bride's parents, Mr. and Mrs. Emil Selig, on East Coast avenue. Rabbi David Marx performed the ceremony in the presence of relatives and intimate friends. The house was artistic with quantities of smilax and vases of pink carnations in all the rooms. The centerpiece of the table in the dining room was a flat basket filled with carnations and ferns. The bride entered with her father and was met by the groom and his best man, Mr. Miton rice of Rochester, NY. The bride's gown was white charmeuse satin, trimmed with princess lace and pearls. Her veil was caught with a wreath of orange blossoms, worn by a sister and her flowers were bride roses showered with lilies of the valley. An informal reception followed the ceremony and Mrs. Selig, mother of the bride, received her wedding guests wearing a gown of lavender chiffon blending into gray, over lavender silk trimmed with lace, and her flowers wour a corsage bouquet of Parma violets. Mrs. R. Frank of Brooklyn, mother of the groom, wore a gray chiffon cloth gown embroidered, trimmed with lace, and folds of coral velvet, and she wore a corsage bouquet of Parma violets. Mrs. M. G. Michale of Athens wore a white lingerie gown over pink silk. Miss. Michael sang several beautiful selections before the ceremony and was accompanied by Miss Regina Silverman, who also played the wedding march. Miss Silverman wore a pink chiffon cloth gown over silk, trimmed with lace and black marabou. The bride's traveling gown was brown velvet with brown chiffon blouse, over Persian silk, and a brown velvet toque trimmed with quills. Mr. and Mrs. Frank are spending several weeks at the Piedmont before going north on a wedding trip. The out of town guests included Mr. and Mrs. R. Frank, of Brooklyn; Mrs. M. G. Michael and Miss Helen Michael, of Athens; Mr. Milton Rce, of Rochester, NY."

After their return from their honeymoon, the couple lived with Lucille's family, and they also became quite active in Atlanta's Jewish community. In 1912, Leo was elected president of the Atlanta chapter of the B'nai B'rith.

During this same time, Mary Phagan began work at the National Pencil Company, still a young teenager. A recent exhibition, "Tragedy in the New South: The Murder of Mary Phagan and the Lynching of Leo Frank," described the conditions Phagan worked in as a child laborer in the factory: "Working conditions in many Southern manufacturing facilities were difficult. Factories were hot in summer, cold in winter, and sanitary conditions were poor. But the issue most prevalent in 1913 was child labor. While most Southern states set a minimum age of twelve for child workers, on April 26, 1913, the Atlanta Georgian reported that Georgia's child labor standards were the nation's worst, with factories employing children as young as ten. The National Pencil Company in Atlanta exemplified these industrial conditions: the factory was supervised by Leo Frank, a Northerner, and Southern girls like Mary Phagan were hired to work low-wage jobs."

Phagan worked in the company's metal room operating a knurling machine, which inserted rubber erasers into the brass bands attached at the end of last-stage production pencils, She worked on average 55 hours a week, for which she was paid $4.05 per week, from the spring of

1912 to April 21, 1913. The metal room was in the section of the factory called the tipping department, across the hallway from Frank's office.

With that, the stage was set for the tragedy that would befall both the 13-year-old Georgia factory girl and the Jewish factory superintendent.

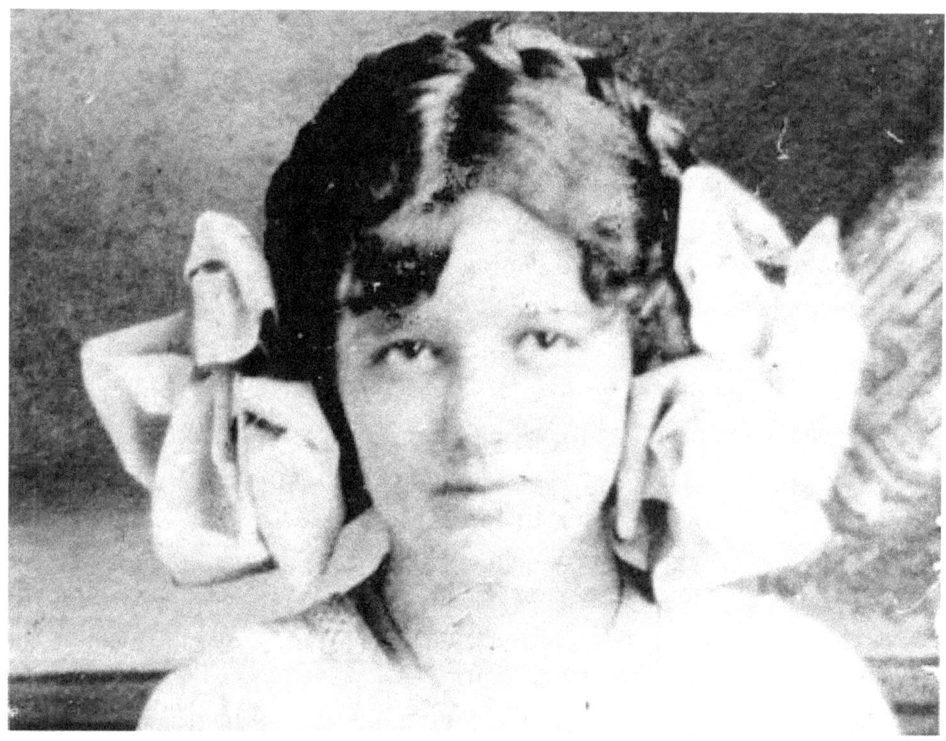

A picture of Phagan shortly before her death

The Murder and Investigation

Phagan was laid off from her job in the tipping department on April 21, 1913, due to a shortage of brass. At noon on April 26, a Saturday being celebrated as Confederate Memorial Day in Georgia. Phagan went to the factory to receive her remaining pay of $1.20. Her mother would later testify, "I last saw her alive on the 26th day of April, 1913, about a quarter to twelve, at home, at 146 Lindsey Street. She was getting ready to go to the pencil factory to get her pay envelope. About 11:30 she ate some cabbage and bread. She left home at a quarter to twelve. She would have been fourteen years old the first day of June, was fair complected, heavy set, very pretty, and was extra large for her age. She had on a lavender dress, trimmed in lace, and a blue hat. She had dimples in her cheeks."

A 14-year-old friend of Phagan's, George Epps, was probably the last person to see her alive. He testified at Frank's trial, "The last time I saw her was Saturday morning coming to town on the English Avenue car. It was about ten minutes to twelve when I first saw her. I left her about seven minutes after twelve at the corner of Forsyth and Marietta Street. She had on that hat, parasol and things when I left her. She was going to the pencil factory to draw her money. She said she was going to see the parade at Elkin-Watson's at two o'clock. She never showed up. I stayed around there until four o'clock and then I went to the ball game. When I left her at the corner of Forsyth and Marietta, I went under the bridge to get papers and she went over the bridge to the pencil factory, about two blocks down Forsyth Street. I sat with Mary on the car."

By the time anyone else saw Mary Phagan, someone had taken her life. Shortly before 3:00 a.m. on the morning of April 27, Newt Lee, the night watchman for the factory, went to the basement to use the bathroom. He later told the court, "I made my rounds regularly every half hour Saturday night. I punched on the hour and punched on the half and I made all my punches. The elevator doors on the street floor and office floor were closed when I got there on Saturday. They were fastened down just like we fasten them down every other night. When three o'clock came I went down the basement and when I went down and got ready to come back I discovered the body there. I went down to the toilet and when I got through I looked at the dust bin back to the door to see how the door was and it being dark I picked up my lantern and went there and I saw something laying there which I thought some of the boys had put there to scare me, then I walked a little piece towards it and I seen what it was and I got out of there. I got up the ladder and called up the police station. It was after three o'clock. I carried the officers down where I found the body."

When the police arrived, they discovered the body of a young girl. Sergeant L. S. Dobbs described what he did and what he saw: "On the morning of April 27th, at about 3:25 a call came from the pencil factory that there was a murder up there. We went down in Boots Rogers' automobile. When we got there the door was locked. We knocked on the door and in about two minutes the negro came down the steps and opened up the door and said there was a woman murdered in the basement. We went through a scuttle hole, a small trapdoor. The negro lead the way back in the basement, to a partition on the left, leading from the elevator. The basement is about twenty feet wide. The negro lead the way back about one hundred fifty feet and we found the body. The girl was lying on her face, not directly lying on her stomach, with the left side on the ground, the right side up just a little. We couldn't tell by looking at her whether she was white or black, only by her golden colored hair. They turned her over and her face was full of dirt and dust. They took a piece of paper and rubbed the dirt off of her face, and we could tell then that it was a white girl. I pulled up her clothes and we could tell by the skin of her knee that she was a white girl. Her face was punctured, full of holes and was swollen and black. She had a cut on the left side of her head as if she had been struck and there was a little blood there. The cord was around her neck, sunk into the flesh. She also had a piece of her underclothing around her neck. The cord was still tight around her neck. The tongue was protruding just the least bit. I began to look around and found a couple of notes. The cord was pulled tight and had cut into the flesh and tied just as tight as it could be. The underclothing around the neck was not tight. There wasn't much blood on her head. It was dry on the outside. I stuck my finger under the hair and it was a little moist. This scratch pad...was also lying on the ground, close to the body. The body was lying with the head towards Forsyth Street, the head being near the partition. I found the notes under the sawdust, lying near the head. The body was that of Mary Phagan. The scratch pad was lying near the notes. They were all right close together."

In the basement, Dobbs testified that her hat was found near the elevator, along with indications that she had been dragged through the dirt and cinder-covered basement floor from the elevator. There was a pile of trash by Phagan's head, and in it the police found two notes that became known as the "murder notes." The first note read, "he said he wood love me land down play like the night witch did it but that long tall black negro did boy his slef." The other said, "mam that negro hire down here did this i went to make water and he push me down that hole a long tall negro black that hoo it wase long sleam tall negro i write while play with me."

In his testimony, Dobbs recalled, "I was reading one of the notes to Lee, with the following words: 'A tall black negro did this, he will try to lay it on the night' and when I got to the word 'night,' Lee says, 'That means the night watchman.' I had just said the 'night' I and he said' That means the night watchman.'"

Based on that, and the fact that Newt Lee seemed to know more about the body than he should have, the police arrested him that morning.

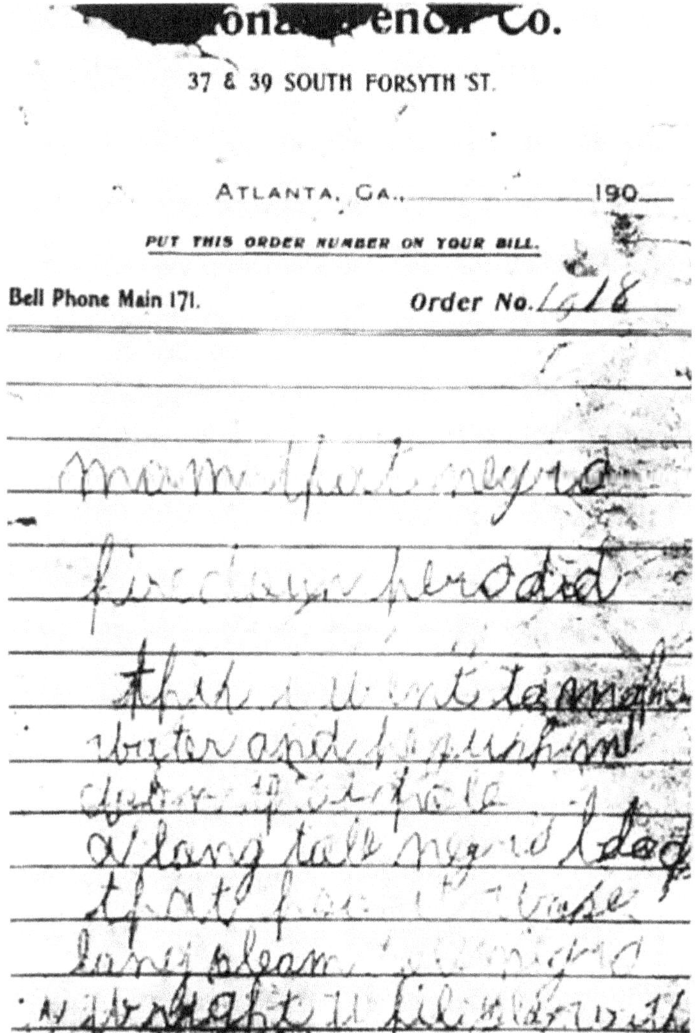

One of the notes

Two different physicians testified at the trial about the condition Phagan's body was found in. County Physician J. W. Hurt examined her on April 27 and reported, "She had a scalp wound on the left side of her head about 21/2 inches long, about 4 inches from the top to the left ear through the scalp to the skull. She had a black contused eye. A number of small minor scratches on the face. The tongue was protruding about a half an inch through the teeth. There was a wound on the left knee, about 2 inches below the knee. There were some superficial scratches on the left and right elbow. There was a cord around the neck and this cord was imbedded into the skin and in my opinion she died from strangulation. This cord...looks like the cord that was around her neck. There was swelling on the neck. In my opinion the cord was put on before death. The wound on the back of the head seemed to have been made with a blunt-edged instrument and the blow from down upward. The scalp wound was made before death. It was calculated to produce unconsciousness. The black eye appeared to have been made by some soft instrument in that the skin was not broken. I think the scratches on the face were made after death. I examined the hymen. It was not intact. There was blood on the drawers. I discovered no violence to the parts. There was blood on the parts. I didn't know whether it was fresh blood or menstrual blood. The vagina was a little larger than the normal size of a girl of that age. It is my opinion that this enlargement of the vagina could have been produced by penetration immediately preceding death."

A later autopsy performed by Dr. H. F. Harris included an examination of Phagan's stomach contents, which confirmed the testimony of Phagan's mother that her last meal consisted of bread and cabbage. He discovered that the food "had progressed very slightly towards digestion. It is impossible for one to say absolutely how long this cabbage had been in the stomach, but I feel confident that she was either killed or received the blow on the back of the head within a half hour after she finished her meal...It is my opinion that she lived from a half to three-quarters of an hour after she ate her meal."

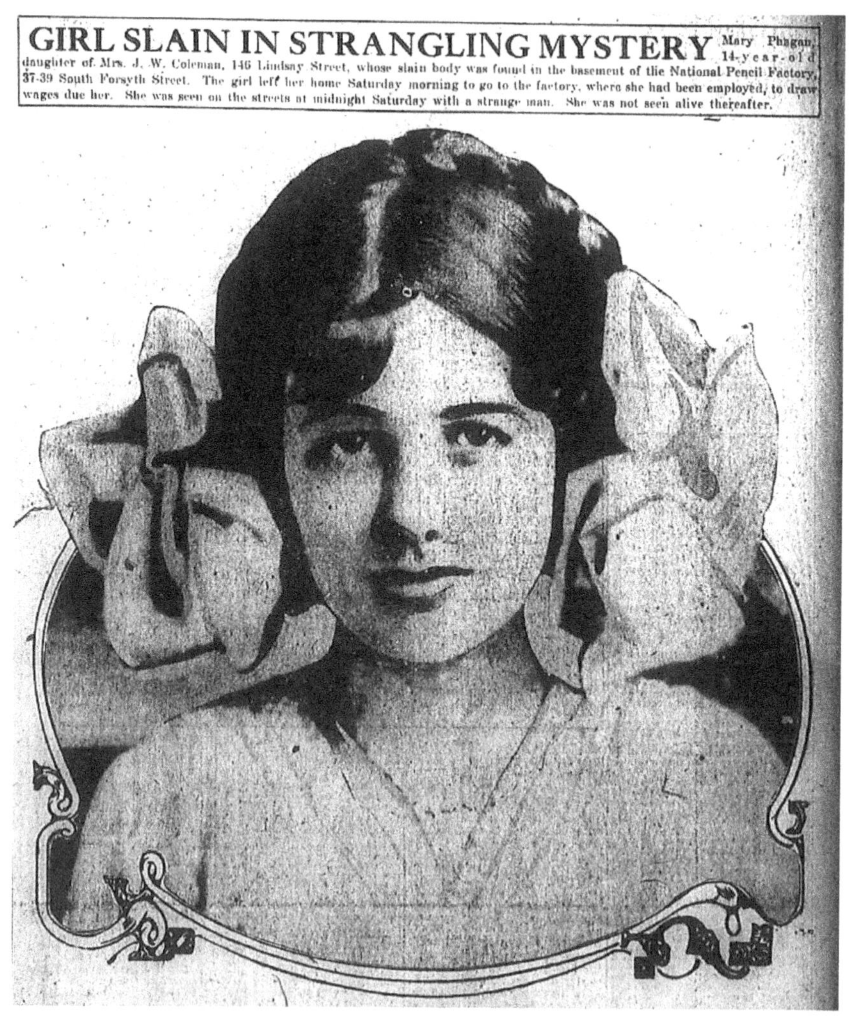

GIRL SLAIN IN STRANGLING MYSTERY Mary Phagan, 14-year-old daughter of Mrs. J. W. Coleman, 146 Lindsay Street, whose slain body was found in the basement of the National Pencil Factory, 37-39 South Forsyth Street. The girl left her home Saturday morning to go to the factory, where she had been employed, to draw wages due her. She was seen on the streets at midnight Saturday with a strange man. She was not seen alive thereafter.

Phagan as depicted in *The Atlanta Journal*

The police continued their investigation at the factory, expanding their search through the complex with the aim of locating the actual scene of the murder. From the evidence they had at that point, it seemed that Phagan had been killed somewhere else and had her body dumped in the basement, so it stood to reason that the crime was committed elsewhere in the building.

During a search of the second floor, attention was drawn to the metal department where Phagan worked. R. P. Barrett was a mechanic at the National Pencil Company, and he testified at Frank's trial about what he discovered the Monday morning after the murder: "I found an unusual spot that I had never seen before at the west end of the dressing room on the second floor of the pencil factory. That spot was not there Friday. The spot was about 4 or 5 inches in diameter and little spots behind these from the rear-6 or 8 in number. I discovered these between 6:30 and 7 o'clock Monday. It was blood. It looked like some white substance had been wiped over it. We kept potash and haskoline, both white substances, on this floor. This white stuff was smeared over the spots. It looked like it had been smeared with a coarse broom. There was a broom on that floor, leaning up against the wall. No, the broom didn't show any evidence of having been used, except that it was dirty. It was used in the metal department for cleaning up the grease. The floor was regularly swept with a broom of finer straw. I found some hair on the handle of a bench lathe. The handle was in the shape of an 'L.' The hair was hanging on the handle, swinging down. Mell Stanford saw this hair. The hair was not there on Friday."

As the investigation went on, the police became convinced that Newt Lee was not the murderer, so they began to consider other likely suspects, including Leo Frank. Frank's behavior immediately after the discovery of Phagan's body was, for lack of a better word, curious. Both Lee and the police tried to call Frank around 4:00 in the morning on Sunday, but they got no answer. Later that morning, Officer J. N. Starnes succeeded in contacting Frank by the phone, and the officer later testified, "I...told him it was very necessary for him to come and if he would come I would send an automobile for him, and I asked Boots Rogers to go for him."

Rogers, the officer dispatched by Starnes to pick up Frank, would tell the court, "It took us five or six minutes to get out to Mr. Frank's residence at 86 E. Georgia Avenue. Mr. Black was with me. Mrs. Frank opened the door. She wore a heavy bathrobe. Mr. Black asked if Mr. Frank was in. Mr. Frank stepped into the hall through the curtain. He was dressed for the street with the exception of his collar, tie, coat and hat. He had on no vest. Mr. Frank asked Mr. Black if anything had happened at the factory. Mr. Black didn't answer. He asked me had anything happened at the factory. I didn't answer. Mr. Frank said, 'Did the night watchman call up and report anything to you?' Mr. Black said, 'Mr. Frank, you had better get your clothes on and let us go to the factory and see what has happened.' Mr. Frank said that he thought he dreamt in the morning about 3 a. m. about hearing the telephone ring. Mr. Black said something about whiskey to Mrs. Frank in Mr. Frank's presence. Mrs. Frank said Mr. Frank hadn't had any breakfast and would we allow him to get breakfast. I told Mr. Black that I was hungry myself. Mr. Frank said let me have a cup of coffee. Mr. Black in a kind of sideways, said, 'I think a drink of whiskey would do him good,' and Mrs. Frank made the remark that she didn't think there was any whiskey in the house. Mr. Frank seemed to be extremely nervous. His questions were jumpy. I never heard him speak in my life until that morning. His voice was a refined voice, it was not coarse. He was rubbing his hands when he came through the curtains. He moved about briskly. He seemed to be excited. He asked questions in rapid succession, but gave plenty of time between questions to have received an answer. Mr. Frank and Mr. Black got on the rear seat and I took the front seat and as I was fixing to turn around, one of us asked Mr. Frank if he knew a little girl by the name of Mary Phagan. Mr. Frank says: 'Does she work at the factory?' and I said, 'I think she does.' Mr. Frank said, 'I cannot tell whether or not she works there until I look on my pay roll book, I know very few of the girls that work there. I pay them off, but I very seldom go back in the factory and I know very few of them, but I can look on my pay roll book and tell you if a girl by the name of Mary Phagan work there.'"

At the factory, according to Rogers' testimony, Frank took the time book out of the safe and looked through it. "Yes," Frank said, "Mary Phagan worked here, she was here yesterday to get her pay." Rogers testified that Frank said to them, "I will tell you about the exact time she left there. My stenographer left about twelve o'clock, and a few minutes after she left the office boy left and Mary came in and got her money and left."

Next, Frank asked to see the crime scene. He accompanied police down to the basement, then showed them through the entire building. Rogers and the other officers recounted that Frank seemed nervous the entire time; John Black, an officer who had accompanied Rogers to the Frank home, claimed that Frank's "voice was hoarse and trembling and nervous and excited. He looked to me like he was pale. I had met Mr. Frank on two different occasions before. On this occasion he seemed to be nervous in handling his collar. He could not get his tie tied, and talked very rapid in asking questions in regard to what had happened."

Despite Frank's obvious discomfort with the situation, police at the time did not consider him a suspect, so he was allowed to return home about 10:45 Sunday morning.

The next day Frank appeared at the police station with his attorney, Luther Rosser. He gave police a written statement about his activities on Saturday, the day Phagan was killed. The statement read, "Saturday April 26th, was a holiday with our company and the factory was shut down. There were several people who came in during the morning. The office boy and the stenographer were in the office with me until noon. They left about 12 or a little after. We have a day watchman there. He left shortly before 12 o'clock. After the office boy and the stenographer left, this little girl, Mary Phagan, came in, but at this time I didn't know that was her name. She came in between 12:05 and 12:10, maybe 12:07, to get her pay envelope...I paid her and she went out of the office. I was in the inner office at my desk...It was impossible to see the direction she went in when she left."

Frank told police he went out for dinner between 1:00 and 3:00. He also mentioned that Newt Lee had arrived at 3:40 and told him to leave and return at 6:00. Frank noted Lee's time card was missing several punches, and that the security guard was supposed to punch in every half hour, but his card for that Saturday had gaps. He said he left the factory at about 6:00, stopped by Jacob's Pharmacy, bought a box of candy for his wife, and arrived home about 6:25. In addition to the statement, Rosser insisted that Frank show police that he had no cuts or injuries. Frank gave police access to the suit he wore on Saturday, and they were unable to find any blood stains, nor were they able to find any blood stains in the laundry at Frank's house.

Nonetheless, by this time, detective John Black had come to believe that Frank was responsible for Phagan's death. He conducted a search of Newt Lee's residence on Tuesday looking for evidence, and in a burn barrel, Black found a shirt with blood smeared high up to the armpits. To police, the shirt look otherwise unused, and Black believed the shirt was planted by the real killer to frame Lee. He further believed that that Frank had planted evidence against Lee, who Black believed was Frank's accomplice in the murder. Based on nothing more than suspicions arising from Frank's nervous behavior during their interviews, police arrested him at the factory around 11:30.

The Atlanta newspapers blared news on Frank's arrest across their front pages. The *Atlanta Journal* reported, "Chief of Detectives N. A. Lanford, announced that L. M. Frank, superintendent of the National Pencil company's factory, where Mary Phagan was found murdered early Sunday morning, would be detained by the police until after the coroner's inquest. The inquest will be resumed Wednesday morning at 9 o'clock. Chief Lanford made this statment when he emerged from a conference which had been in progress in his office on the third floor of the police station since shortly after 1 o'clock….Chief Lanford declared that the police were working on the theory that the murder mystery could be cleared up through evidence which they hope to obtain from the negro night watchman and from Mr. Frank. He said that the detectives had been unable to find any credible evidence to the effect that the girl ever had been seen since she entered the factory about noon last Saturday to get her wages."

As police held Frank and a coroner's inquest was opened on April 30, Mary Phagan was laid to rest. The *Atlanta Constitution* described the funeral vividly: "While relatives hysterically wept, while hundreds of friends with wet eyes and bowed heads, mourned, while little circles of grim visaged men talked in hushed voices…all that remained of little 14-year-old Mary Phagan, victim of Saturday night's atrocious crime, was lowered into a grave at the city cemetery at Marietta yesterday morning. 'The Lord hath given, the Lord hath taken, blessed be the name of the Lord,' said Rev. T. T. G. Linkous, pastor of the Christian church at East Point, as tears streamed down his cheeks, And the grave-diggers grasped their spades and filled the grave. When the sad little funeral party arrived in Marietta with the casket shortly before 10 o'clock, there was a great crowd at the station to meet them. With solemn mien, hundreds of men and women, girls and boys, followed the train of carriages to the Second Baptist church. So unstrung was everyone connected with the tragedy that no details had been looked after. It was upon the church grounds that the pallbearers...were selected. With the little white casket on their shoulder, they walked into the tiny country church...With voices that cracked because of choked back tears, yet were sacred because of the feeling behind them, the choir sang 'Rock of Ages.' A dozen times during every stanza they were interrupted by the wailings of the bereaved mother. 'The light of my life has been taken. Oh, god, and her soul was as pure and as white as her body,' she sobbed incoherently. No attempt was made to stop her."

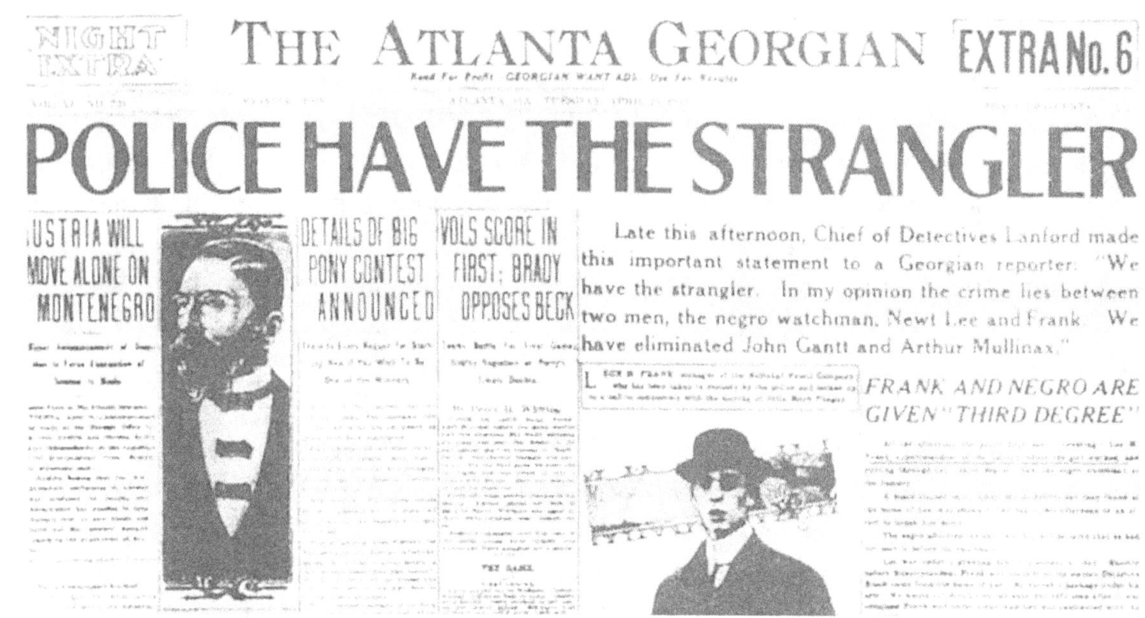

A picture of *The Atlanta Georgian* headline on April 29, 1913

The coroner's inquest began in Atlanta the same day as Phagan's funeral. Frank testified about his activities on that Saturday, and his testimony was corroborated by other witnesses. There was no physical evidence or even circumstantial clues that pointed to Frank as the guilty party, but several witnesses provided testimony that brought Frank's character into question, particularly his treatment of the young women who worked at the factory. One young man testified that Phagan had complained that Frank had been flirting with her. The *Atlanta Constitution* told readers, "Evidence that Leo M. Frank, superintendent of the pencil factory in which the lifeless body of Mary Phagan was found, had tried to flirt with her, and that she was growing afraid of his advances, was submitted to the coroner's jury at the inquest yesterday afternoon, a short time before adjournment was taken until 4:30 o'clock today by George W. Epps, aged 15, a chum of the murdered victim. George rode with Mary to the city Saturday morning an hour before she disappeared at noon. He testified late Wednesday afternoon that the girl had told him of attempts Leo Frank had made to flirt with her, and of apparent advances in which he was growing bolder. 'She said she was getting afraid,' he told at the inquest. 'She wanted me to come to the factory every afternoon in the future and escort her home. She didn't like the way Mr. Frank was acting toward her.'"

The inquest continued through the first week of May, and during this time, the atmosphere in

Atlanta still remained relatively calm. The *Atlanta Constitution* ran an editorial under the headline "Keep an Open Mind." Its author wrote, "Sooner or later the 'murder will out,' but the verdict must come in an orderly and a legal way, and until something more definite develops than has yet been ascertained it is the duty of the public to keep an open mind. Nothing can be more unjust nor more repugnant to the popular sense of justice than to convict even by hearsay an innocent man. The Constitution, therefore, takes this occasion to call upon the public to suspend judgement and not to endeavor to convict even by indirection, anyone who has not had the full and fair showing guaranteed by the constitution of the state and of the United States, not to speak of the all-pervading guarantee that the public's sense of justice should throw around any man who, by law, is presumed to be innocent until he is proven to be guilty. We say this without reference to any individual, but in justice to all who are even indirectly under suspicion."

After hearing the evidence and the testimony of witnesses, the coroner's jury delivered its verdict on May 8: "We, the coroner's jury, empaneled and sworn by Paul Donehoo, coroner of Fulton County, to inquire into the death of Mary Phagan, whose dead body now lies before us, after having heard the evidence of sworn witnesses, and the statement of Dr. J. W. Hurt, County Physician, find that the deceased came to her death from strangulation. We recommend that Leo M. Frank and Newt Lee be held under charges of murder for further investigation by the Fulton County grand jury."

That conclusion was rendered despite the fact that a week earlier, while Frank and Lee were being held in custody, another person of interest emerged. On May 1, police arrested Jim Conley, the janitor at the pencil factory, after he had been observed washing red stains out of a blue work shirt. Conley claimed it was rust, and when police tested the stains and found it was in fact rust, they returned the shirt, but Conley remained in police custody for two weeks. This took place during the coroner's inquest, but Conley was never called to testify.

While in custody, Conley gave a statement saying that he had been visiting saloons, shooting dice, and drinking on the day of the murder, but detectives found a witness who told them that "a black negro...dressed in dark blue clothing and hat" had been seen in the lobby of the factory on the day of the murder. Moreover, when detectives determined Conley could read and write, they examined his handwriting and determined there were similarities between his spelling and the spelling found on the murder notes. Conley admitted on May 24 that he had written the notes, but he insisted he did so at Frank's direction on the day before Mary Phagan's murder, which not only implicated Frank but indicated that the crime was premeditated. Then, in a second affidavit, Conley claimed he lied about the meeting on Friday. According to the second account, Frank had met him in the street on Saturday, had Conley follow him to the factory, and dictated the notes that day.

importance that they could prove against the negro, and you may be sure they left no stone unturned. Then, what is the gist of his evidence?

It is, that he saw two girls go up stairs, and only one come down: Mary went first, and Monteen followed; and Monteen remained up head of the stairs, looking wild and excited; and that Frank asked him if he had seen a girl come up stairs, and Jim answered, "I seed two go up, but I ain't seen but one come down."

Then Frank told him that he had tried Mary in the metal room, and that she had resisted, and he had struck her, and "I guess I hit her

JIM CONLEY.

stairs quite a little bit, and then came back down and went away; and that he had already heard steps like two persons walking back to the metal room, just before Monteen came in; and that, after Monteen left, some one came running to the front up stairs on tip-toes; and then he heard the "stomp" that Frank always made when he was signalling Jim about a woman; and that he answered the signal, and found Frank near the too hard;" and that she had struck something as she fell.

Frank told the negro he must help get the body to the basement; and the negro went to where the girl was lying on her back, with hands and arms *up*.

Frank had torn a strip from her underclothing, had folded it, and had placed it under her head—and that blood-clotted piece of undergarment had its tremendous weight with the

Conley

   While the police were interviewing Conley and receiving different stories from him, a Fulton County grand jury had been meeting to consider evidence in the Phagan murder. The grand jury convened on May 23, with Hugh Dorsey, the prosecutor, presenting evidence. Dorsey presented the minimal amount of evidence necessary for the grand jury to consider an indictment, promising jurors that more information would be presented at trial.

   The grand jury issued an indictment on May 24: "In the name and behalf of the citizens of Georgia, charge and accuse Leo M. Frank, of the [Fulton] County and State [of Georgia] aforesaid, with the offense of Murder, for that the said Leo M. Frank in the County aforesaid on the 26th day of April in the year of our Lord nineteen hundred and thirteen, with force and arms did unlawfully and with malice aforethought kill and murder one Mary Phagan by then and there choking her, the said Mary Phagan, with a cord place around her neck contrary to the laws of said State, the good order, peace and dignity thereof."

The *Atlanta Constitution* reported, "In discussing the time of Frank's trial, [Dorsey] stated that he could not say when it would be started. 'It will not be possible to hold it before the latter part of June,' he asserted, 'and whether or not it is held then depends on a number of things. I have much work to do to get the case ready and there is also the defense to be considered, as they may secure additional time.'"

Dorsey

Meanwhile, police were trying to get Conley's story on a firmer foundation. When Conley's second story was reported, some officials at the pencil company contended that Conley, not Frank, was the actual murderer of Phagan. They believed Conley was trying to frame Frank for the crime, which they figured was a robbery gone bad. The police, in an attempt to resolve doubts concerning Conley's testimony, attempted to arrange a confrontation between Frank and Conley on May 28. Frank, whose lawyer was out of town, refused the meeting, and police told the *Atlanta Constitution* that they considered this tantamount to an admission of guilt.

Conley was further interviewed by police on May 24, and the third affidavit he provided was by far the most damning for Frank. The entire statement was published on the front page of the *Atlanta Journal* and quoted extensively in the *Atlanta Constitution*. In this third affidavit, Conley told police that "when I came back to the pencil factory with Mr. Frank I waited for him downstairs like he told me, and when he whistled for me I went upstairs and he asked me if I wanted to make some money right quick, and I told him yes, sir, and he told me that he had picked up a girl back there and had let her fall and that her head hit against something--he didn't know what it was--and for me to move her and I hollered and told him the girl was dead. And he told me to pick her up and bring her to the elevator, and I told him I didn't have nothing to pick her up with, and he told me to go and look by the cotton box there and get a piece of cloth and I got a wide piece of cloth and come back there to the men's toilet, where she was, and tied her, and I taken her and brought her up there to a little dressing room carrying her on my right shoulder and fell on the floor right there at the dressing room and I hollered for Mr. Frank to come there and help me, that she was too heavy for me, and Mr. Frank came down there and told me to pick her up, dam fool, and he run down there to me and he was excited, and he picked her up by the feet."

Conley described how they got her on the elevator to the basement and placed Phagan on the floor of the basement where she would later be found: "Mr Frank joined me back of the elevator and he stepped on the elevator when it go to where he was, and he said, 'Gee, that was a tiresome job.'"

According to Conley, they returned to the second floor, and Frank "then asked me to write a few lines on that paper, a white scratch pad he had there and he told me what to put on there and I asked him what he was going to do with it and he told me to just go ahead and write, and then after I got through writing Mr. Frank looked at it and said it was all right, and Mr. Frank looked up at the top of the house and said, 'Why should I hang? I have wealthy people in Brooklyn,' and I asked him what about me and he told me that was all right about me for me to keep my mouth shut and he would make everything alright...The reason I have not told this before is I thought Mr. Frank would get out and help me out, but it seems that he is not going to get out, and I decided to tell the whole truth about the matter."

Conley concluded by claiming that Frank gave him $200, but then took it back and said, "Let me have that and I will make it alright with you Monday if I live and nothing happens."

Conley's affidavit, describing Frank's hiding of the body and his behavior, caused an immediate sensation in Atlanta, though some cautioned that the statements only added to the confusion and mystery surrounding Phagan's murder. The *Atlanta Constitution* sounded a moderate tone: "Amid the warp of falsehood and the woof of conjecture, one thing stands out like a scarlet thread in the Mary Phagan murder mystery--for mystery it still is and still will be until a jury of twelve men fixes the guilt on some man or men. That one thing--startling in its vivid contrast to the murky maze of contradictions--is the fact that James conley, the nego sweeper employed at the National Pencil factory, wrote the notes which were found beside the mutilated and lifeless body of Mary Phagan early in the morning of April 26. Why he wrote them, when he wrote them, whether he wrote at the dictation of someone else or whether he himself committed the crime are matters yet to be determined...He tells various stories about the writing of the notes. He puts improbable words in the mouth of Leo Frank."

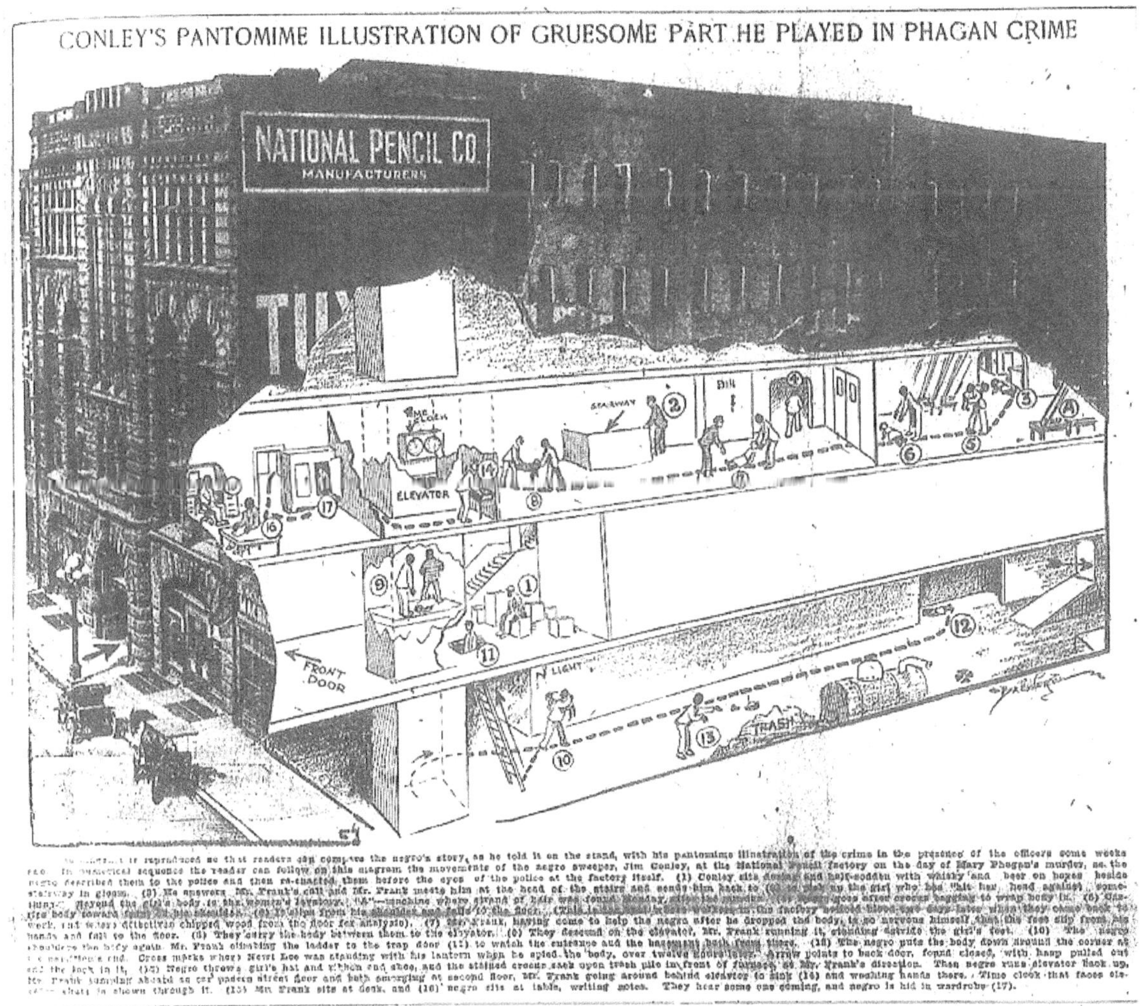

The Atlanta Journal's depiction of the crime according to Conley

The *Atlanta Journal* took the unusual move of publishing two parallel analyses, one pointing out the weaknesses in Conley's story and the other noting the reasonable aspects of the story. The paper explained, "Below are given the analyses of the negro, James Conley's latest statement or confession from two viewpoints. In one analysis the negro's statement is weighed with the idea that Conley has not told the whole truth, that he is endeavoring to hide his own responsibility in an accusation of Mr. Frank, who is innocent of the crime, is the victim of a chain of circumstances which link his name with suspicion. In the other analysis Conley's confession is discussed from the standpoint of the man who regards it as being truthful and its points are argued from that partisan angle. The Journal presents these discussions without any with to influence any reader to either view but simply for whatever news value they may have in throwing light on the case."

Much was made of the fact that Conley was black, and that he was accusing Frank, a white man, of the crime. What was missing from the coverage and the rhetoric up to this point was mention of Frank's Jewish heritage. At this point, anti-Semitism was not part of the atmosphere surrounding the case.

The Trial

Frank's trial began on July 28, 1913 in the Fulton County Superior Court. The prosecution was led by Dorsey, and it included William Smith as his jury consultant. Frank was represented by a team of eight attorneys and jury selection specialists led by Luther Rosser, Reuben Arnold, and Herbert Haas. The courtroom was crowded, with hundreds of spectators both inside and outside the courthouse. The defense would later claim that the witnesses and the jury were intimidated by the crowds into convicting Frank.

Rosser

Frank in the courtroom

A newspaper depiction of the jurors

Over the course of the next three weeks, the jury and court spectators would hear dozens of witnesses testify and discussion over the physical evidence. Conley was the star witness for the prosecution, and the defense was unable to produce holes in his account over the course of 16 hours of cross examination spread over 3 days.

Dorsey also called witnesses to testify concerning the blood stains and strands of hair found in the metal room, pointing to it as evidence in support of the prosecution's theory that the murder occurred outside of Frank's office on the second floor. The defense disputed this, arguing that the hair and blood may not have been Phagan's, and that given the fact the machines were worked by young women about Phagan's age and injuries were not uncommon, the blood and hair could have come from any of them. Moreover, the material used to strangle Phagan was present throughout the factory.

Other pieces of evidence were also heavily contested. Dorsey forcefully insisted the physical evidence supported Conley's story that he and Frank carried Phagan's body from the second floor to the elevator, then from the elevator to where the body was found. The defense argued the drag marks on the floor of the basement indicated that Conley carried Phagan's body down to the basement by ladder, then dragged her across the floor. In addition, the defense argued that Conley was the murderer, not Frank, and that the two murder notes were written by Conley with Newt Lee's help. The defense also pointed to Phagan's missing purse as evidence in support of their contention that Conley murdered Phagan as part of a robbery gone wrong.

A courtroom photo from July 28, 1913 of Newt Lee testifying

With the physical evidence in dispute, the question of motive came to the fore. The defense's contention, that Conley murdered Phagan as part of a robbery, was one that was easy to make to a white jury in early 20th century Georgia. The defense played to the jury's prejudices in portraying Phagan as the victim of a treacherous, thieving black man.

In further support of Frank's innocence, the defense called young women who worked at the factory to testify about his good behavior. The *Atlanta Constitution* told readers, "Numbers of girls and women, either now employed or formerly employed at the National Pencil factory, were placed on the stand Monday by the defense to swear to the good character of Superintendent Leo M. Frank...Mrs. Mattie Thompson, a woman of over middle age and an employee of the factory, was among those put on the stand to testify to Leo Frank's character and also about the alleged flirting carried on by some of the girls from the windows of the dressing rooms. She said that she did not know the names of any of them and had never seen any of them in the act of carrying on a flirtation, but that it had been talked of in the factory and she and some of the other elderly ladies had reported it to N. V. Darley, assistant superintendent. She said Frank's character was good."

For its part, the prosecution argued that Frank preyed on the young women who worked in the factory. The state alleged that he regularly met with girls in his office and had sexual relations with them, and Dorsey called witnesses who testified about Frank's alleged behavior. The *Atlanta Constitution* reported, "Solicitor Dorsey made a persistent effort Wednesday morning to show that the character of Leo Frank is anything but good. He laid particular stress on his character as to his relations with women and girls, and introduced a large number of women who testified that in this respect his character was in their judgement bad."

One witness, a former factory employee named Willie Turner, testified that, contrary to Frank's contention he was unfamiliar with Phagan to police the morning her body was found, Frank did know Phagan. In fact, according to Turner, he had seen Frank with Phagan in the metal room. He told the court, "I saw Leo Frank talking to Mary Phagan on the second floor, about the middle of March. It was just before dinner. There was nobody else in the room then. She was going to work and he stopped to talk to her. She told him she had to go to work. He told her that he was the superintendent of the factory, and that he wanted to talk to her, and she said she had to go to work. She backed off and he went on towards her talking to her. The last thing I heard him say was he wanted to talk to her. That is all I saw or heard."

Another factory girl, Ruth Robinson, testified, "I have seen Leo M. Frank talking to Mary Phagan. He was talking to her about her work, not very often. He would just tell her, while she was at work, about her work. He would stand just close enough to her to tell her about her work. He would show her how to put rubbers in the pencils. He would just take up the pencil and show her how to do it. That's all I saw him do. I heard him speak to her; he called her Mary. That was last summer."

Dewey Hewell had worked at the Pencil Factory in early 1913 before quitting in March of that year, and she told the court, "I have seen Mr. Frank talk to Mary Phagan two or three times a day in the metal department. I have seen him hold his hand on her shoulder. He called her Mary. He would stand pretty close to her. He would lean over in her face."

After almost a month of testimony, the defense and prosecution made their closing arguments. Dorsey summed up the prosecution argument for Frank's guilt over the course of two days, emphasizing the physical evidence that could implicate Frank, the testimony concerning his actions, the witnesses who had testified to his lascivious character, and Frank's own nervousness before his arrest. In conclusion, Dorsey railed, "Gentlemen, every act of that defendant proclaims him guilty. Gentlemen, every word of that defendant proclaims him responsible for the death of this little factory girl. Gentlemen, every circumstances in this case proves him guilty of this crime. Extraordinary? Yes, but nevertheless true, just as true as Mary Phagan is dead. She died a noble death, not a blot on her name. She died because she wouldn't yield her virtue to the demands of her superintendent. I have no purpose and have never had from the beginning in this case that you oughtn't have, as an honest, upright citizen of this community. In the language of Daniel Webster, I desire to remind you 'that when a jury, through whimsical and unfounded scruples, suffers the guilty to escape, they make themselves answerable for the augmented danger to the innocent.' Your Honor, I have done my duty. I have no apology to make. Your Honor, so far as the State is concerned, may now charge this jury, this jury who have sworn that they were impartial and unbiased, this jury who, in this presence, have taken the oath that they would well and truly try the issue formed on this bill of indictment between the State of Georgia and Leo M. Frank, charged with the murder of Mary Phagan; and I predict, may it please Your Honor, that under the law that you give in charge and under the honest opinion of the jury of the evidence produced, there can be but one verdict, and that is: We the jury find the defendant, Leo M. Frank, guilty! GUILTY! GUILTY!"

Frank's defense attorneys requested a mistrial, arguing that the jurors had been intimidated by the crowd inside and outside the courtroom, but Judge Roan denied the motion. In his summation before the jury, Rosser called into question the truthfulness and reliability of the state's star witness, Conley, and the actions of the state in their investigation of the crime. He also explicitly raised the specter of anti-Semitism in the fact that Frank had been arrested in the first place: "Gentlemen, take a look at this spectacle, if you can. Here is a Jewish boy from the north. He is unacquainted with the south. He came here alone and without friends and he stood alone. This murder happened in his place of business...He is defenseless and helpless. He knows his innocence and is willing to find the murderer. They try to place the murder on him. God, all merciful and all powerful, look upon a scene like this!"

Rosser concluded, "Believe Frank was in the factory if you can at 1:30; throw aside all the respectable people and swear by Conley. Well, I know the American jury is supreme, that it is the sovereign over lives; that sometimes you can sway it by passion and prejudice, but you can't make it believe anything like this. Neither prejudice, nor passion, wrought by monsters so vile they ought not to be in the court room, could make them believe it...Gentlemen, I want only the straight truth here, and I have yet to believe that the truth has to be watched and cultivated by these detectives and by seven visits of the solicitor general. I don't believe any man, no matter what his rate, ought to be tried under such testimony. If I was raising sheep and feared for my lambs, I might hang a yellow dog on it. I might do it in the daytime, but when things got quiet at night and I got to thinking, I'd be ashamed of myself. You have been overly kind to me, gentlemen. True, you have been up against a situation like that old Sol Russell used to describe when he would say, 'Well, I've lectured off and on for forty years, and the benches always stuck it out, but they was screwed to the floor.' You gentlemen have been practically in that fix, but I feel, nevertheless, that you have been peculiarly kind, and I thank you."

The case went to the jury on August 25, 1913, and because he feared for Frank's safety if he was found not guilty, Judge Roan allowed the defendant and his attorneys to be absent from the courtroom when the verdict was read. After only four hours of deliberation, the jury returned and announced a verdict of guilty. The *Atlanta Constitution* described the scene: "At 4 minutes to 5 o'clock a jury of his peers filed slowly into the courtroom, which for four weeks has been the scene of the greatest legal battle in the history of the state. The room had been cleared of the morbidly curious who for days have listened to the fierce fight for and against the young man. Only the newspaper men, Sheriff Magnum, his deputies, Solicitor Dorsey and Frank Hooper, a few lawyers and some close personal friends of the defendant were in the room. On the face of each juror was the drawn look of men who had been compelled, through duty, to do an awful thing--to consign a fellow creature to the gallows. There was no mistaking that look. The strongest of the men shook as if some strange ailment had stricken them. It took no student of human nature to read that the verdict was the ultimate one of guilt. A hush fell over the courtroom. The scraping of a chair across the floor, the rustle of a fan, the shuffling of a foot would have been welcome sounds. The silence was fearsome. Slowly, with a voice that trembled, Fred Winburn, foreman of the jury, read the verdict. Immediately there was the hustle and bustle of reporters and strident voices calling out 'guilty' over the telephones to Atlanta's three newspapers. The sound reached the street below and a shout went up from the waiting mob outside. The end had come to the longest criminal trial on record in this state."

The *Constitution* summed up what was left for Frank after the verdict: "There are but two courses that Frank may now pursue to regain his life and his freedom, and these may do nothing more than postpone the effect of the verdict of the present jury. Frank may ask for a new trial, and in case this is not granted they may appeal to the higher court. Should the higher court grant this new trial he has one more chance: should it not, he must die unless the governor should see fit to interfere."

Judge Roam summoned both prosecution and defense attorneys to his chambers the next day, August 26, and formally pronounced a sentence of death by hanging, setting the date of October 10.

Judge Roan

A Shameful End

From nearly the moment Frank's death sentence was announced, the defense began immediately to appeal the verdict. In a public protest, they made the argument that public opinion had swayed the jury against Frank. As a show of support, that September, the Atlanta chapter of B'nai B'rith unanimously reelected Frank as its president, an indication that he still had the backing of Atlanta's Jewish community.

The first step in the appeal was a reconsideration of the case by the original trial judge, because according to Georgia law at the time, death penalty cases could only be appealed based on errors of law, not on reconsideration of the evidence. Frank's attorneys argued in writing to Judge Roan that there had been 115 procedural problems with the trial, including jury prejudice and intimidation by the crowds both in and out of the courtroom.

After consideration of the arguments and the testimony of witnesses, including the jurors themselves, Judge Roan denied the defense's motion for a new trial. In his statement, he explained, "I have thought about this case more than any other I have ever tried. With all the thought I have put on this case, I am not thoroughly convinced that Frank is guilty or innocent. But I do not have to be convinced. The jury was convinced. There is no room to doubt that."

Frank next appealed to the Georgia Supreme Court. On December 15, each side was granted two hours for oral arguments in addition to presenting the existing written record. The defense reiterated the arguments it made before Judge Roan and included reservations the judge expressed during the reconsideration. The prosecution argued that the evidence convicting Frank was overwhelming, and that Roan's doubts were irrelevant. On February 17, 1914, in a 4-2 decision, the Georgia Supreme Court denied Frank a new trial, with the majority dismissing the defense's allegations of bias. The dissenting judges concluded that Conley's evidence had prejudiced the jurors and denied Frank a fair trial. They wrote, "It is perfectly clear to us that evidence of prior bad acts of lasciviousness committed by the defendant...did not tend to prove a preexisting design, system, plan, or scheme, directed toward making an assault upon the deceased or killing her to prevent its disclosure."

With Frank's last regular state appeal having run its course, Frank's execution was set for April 17, 1914. The defense, however, continued to work on his behalf, including filing an extraordinary motion with the Georgia Supreme Court raising facts not available at the original trial. The appeal was heard by Justice Benjamin Hill, beginning on April 23, 1914.

Among other issues raised by defense was the repudiation in a newspaper interview by a state biologist of his identification of the hair found on the lathe in the metal room as Phagan's. The defense also included evidence that the murder letters were composed by Conley in the basement rather than Frank's office, and the defense enclosed prison letters written by Conley to Annie Maude Carter which, the defense argued, implicated Conley as the murderer. In addition, the defense argued that Frank's absence from the court deprived the defendant of due process under the law.

For every issue raised by the defense, the state had a response, and Hill ultimately denied Frank a new trial, a decision upheld by the rest of the Georgia Supreme Court on November 14, 1914. In their denial, it found that the due process argument had been raised too late in the process, and that it should have first been considered by Roan during his review.

While Frank's defense team was taking his case through the courts, there was a battle raging in the press over whether Frank was actually guilty. On March 14, 1914, the *Atlanta Journal* came out in support of a new trial for Frank, but into the fray leapt Tom Watson, the former Populist Party candidate for president and editor of the *Jeffersonian*. Watson had remained silent during the Frank trial, but after the *Journal* came out in support of Frank, Watson published a furious defense of the state's prosecution of Frank on March 19: "Leo Frank was accused of the murder of Mary Phagan, one of the numerous girls who, for a mere pittance, worked under him at a pencil factory. Upon the fiendish brutalities that were practiced upon the little victim, I need not dwell. Upon what has been said and proven about Frank's abnormal sexuality, I will not comment. Upon the decadent and satyr-like features--eyes, lips and jaw--that Nature gave him, it might not be fair to remark. It is sufficient to say that any trained lawyer who followed the evidence in the case, ad delivered in court, must have reached the conclusion, by a process of elimination, that the hideous crimes perpetrated upon the poor little girl were either the joint acts of Frank and the negro, Conley; or, were the acts of the one with the connivance of the other. From the sworn testimony before the jury, it was utterly impossible for them to have reached any other verdict."

Watson included explicitly anti-Semitic statements in the article: "Is Frank better than anybody else? Does a Jew expect extraordinary favors and immunities, because of his race? In this case, the defendant is taking that position. Anyone who has noticed the New York papers, has noticed the persistent efforts made from Atlanta to arouse the Hebrews into believing that Frank is a victim of race prejudice. Is it wise for the Jews to risk the good name and popularity of the whole race in the extraordinary, extra-judicial, and utterly unprecedented methods that are being worked to save this decadent offshoot of a great people?"

Watson

Over the course of the next year, Watson's publication became consumed with the Frank case, and its tone became increasingly anti-Semitic. Among the articles Watson wrote and published was one on July 15, 1915 entitled "While Leo Frank is Loafing at the State Farm, the Rich Jews are Continuing to Defame the People and the Courts of Georgia."

After the denial of the extraordinary appeal to the Georgia Supreme Court, Frank's legal team brought an appeal to the U.S. Supreme Court. His attorney's request for a writ of error based on Frank's absence from the jury verdict was denied, first by Justice Joseph Lamar and then Justice Oliver Wendell Holmes Jr., who concluded that the issue had been raised too late. The full Supreme Court heard the request and denied the motion without issuing an opinion, though Holmes did write in a dissent, "I very seriously doubt if the petitioner ... has had due process of law ... because of the trial taking place in the presence of a hostile demonstration and seemingly dangerous crowd, thought by the presiding Judge to be ready for violence unless a verdict of guilty was rendered."

Buoyed by that, Frank's lawyers filed a motion for a writ of habeas corpus, and in the motion they argued that it was the threat of crowd violence that forced Frank's absence and constituted a violation of due process. On April 19, 1915, in a 7-2 decision in the case *Frank v. Mangum*, the Supreme Court denied the appeal, basing its decision on the timeliness issue. Holmes and Chief Justice Charles Evans Hughes dissented, with Holmes writing the dissent. In it, he wrote, "It is our duty to declare lynch law as little valid when practiced by a regularly drawn jury as when administered by one elected by a mob intent on death."

Holmes, Jr.

Chief Justice Hughes

With all judicial appeals exhausted, Frank turned back to the state and the only avenues he had remaining to avoid the death penalty. On April 22, 1915, the Georgia Prison Commission received an application for the commutation of Frank's death sentence, but it rejected the petition on June 9. Frank's only hope now rested with Georgia Governor John Slaton.

Governor Slaton

Slaton's term was up four days after Frank's scheduled execution, but the governor had a potential conflict of interest: in 1913 he had merged his law practice with Luther Rosser, who led Frank's defense team. Slaton had no role in the original trial, but partisans against Frank such as Watson pointed to the partnership to question Slaton's consideration of Frank's petition.

Governor Slaton began hearing evidence on June 12 in the form of presentations from both the state and the defense, including new arguments and evidence. He visited the crime scene and reviewed some 10,000 pages of documents. Among the documents was a letter written by Judge Roan to Frank's lawyers in December 1914, shortly before he died: "After considering your communication...I wish to say, that at the proper time, I shall ask the Prison Commission to recommend, and the Governor to commute Frank's sentence to life imprisonment. This, however, I will not do until the defendant's application shall have been filed and the Governor and Prison Commission shall have had opportunity to study the record in the case. It is possible that I showed undue deference to the opinion of the jury in this case, when I allowed their verdict to stand. They said by their verdict that they had found the truth. I was still in a state of uncertainty, and so expressed myself...After many months of continued deliberations I am still uncertain of Frank's guilt. This state of uncertainty is largely due to the character of the Negro Conley's testimony, by which the verdict was evidently reached. Therefore I consider this a case in which the chief magistrate of the state should exert every effort in ascertaining the truth."

After reviewing the evidence, Slaton issued a 29-page report that defended the trial court's guilty verdict and criticized outsiders for their criticism of Georgia and its court system. He insisted the state's evidence presented of Frank's guilt was reasonable and comprehensive, including Conley's testimony, though he did call into question the totality of Conley's testimony, focusing on inconsistencies he had discovered in Conley's description of moving the body to the basement and the writing of the murder notes. Based on his full consideration of the original record and new evidence that had been developed, Slaton commuted Frank's conviction to life imprisonment on June 21, 1915.

News of the commutation hit Georgia like a bomb. The public, which had been whipped into a frenzy against Frank through the intemperate writings of Watson and others, was outraged. A mob threatened to storm the Governor's Mansion, requiring the Georgia National Guard to disperse the angry crowd. Frank was moved to the Milledgeville State Penitentiary under the cover of darkness for his own protection, but another prisoner attacked Frank on July 17, nearly severing his jugular vein in the process.

Watson, who had seen circulation of *The Jeffersonian* skyrocket thanks to his articles about Frank, began advocating that Georgians take the law into their own hands. In one article, he wrote, "This country has nothing to fear from its rural communities. Lynch law is a good sign; it shows that a sense of justice lives among the people."

In response to such calls, a group calling itself the "Knights of Mary Phagan" planned to kidnap Frank and lynch him. On August 16, 1915 the lynch mob attacked the prison, grabbed Frank, and drove away. At Frey's Gin, two miles east of Marietta, a site for the hanging had been prepared. Frank was handcuffed, his legs were tied at the ankles, and he was hanged from the branch of a tree around 7:00 in the morning on August 17.

The mob action elicited immediate outrage from around the country. The *Atlanta Journal* termed the lynching "Georgia's Shame":

> "In that act the sovereignty of the state of Georgia has been assaulted, desecrated, raped. No word in the language is too strong to apply to the deliberate and carefully conspired deed of the mob. The assault of the lowest criminal upon the life, person or property of another affects directly but two persons, the assailant and his victim; that act of the mob which lynched Leo Frank has put a stain upon the escutcheon of a state which more than 2,500,000 people are trying to preserve untarnished...It is...the duty of the constituted state authorities now, first to find and place the responsibility for the carrying off and lynching of this prisoner, and the wanton assault upon the law; second to search out and locate each and every member of that lawless mob and administer merited punishment for a deed that has hanged a millstone around the neck of Georgia."

This proved to be wishful thinking. Despite the fact that various members of the Knights of Mary Phagan were well known (including former Georgia Governor Joseph Mackey Brown), and even though numerous photographs clearly showing members of the lynch mob were circulated in newspapers around the country, no one was ever arrested for Frank's murder. In fact, postcards of the lynching became popular souvenirs around the region.

Brown

A picture of the lynching, with Judge Newt Morris in a straw hat on the right

Other pictures of the lynching

A postcard of the lynching

Frank's body was eventually cut down and transported to Atlanta, and the funeral home where his body lay was besieged by thousands demanding to see his corpse. He was then transported from Atlanta to New York by train. He was buried in the Mount Carmel Cemetery, Glendale, Queens, New York on August 20, 1915.

In the decades after Frank's lynching, the consensus among historians grew that he had been wrongly convicted. Most historians now believe that Conley was solely responsible for Mary Phagan's murder. The movement for a posthumous pardon of Frank began almost immediately after his death, but it was not until 1982 that a formal request was made to the Georgia State Board of Pardons and Paroles. This request was made by Charles Wittenstein and Dale Swartz, based on an interview given to *The Tennessean* by Alonzo Mann, Frank's office boy, who said he had seen Conley carrying Phagan's body through the lobby of the factory toward a ladder to the basement. The Board reviewed the trial record and files from Governor Slaton's commutation, but in the end it denied the request. According to the Board, "After exhaustive review and many hours of deliberation, it is impossible to decide conclusively the guilt or innocence of Leo M. Frank. For the board to grant a pardon, the innocence of the subject must be shown conclusively."

In 1986, however, Frank supporters filed another application, this time asking the state of Georgia to recognize its role in his lynching. The pardon was granted: "Without attempting to address the question of guilt or innocence, and in recognition of the State's failure to protect the person of Leo M. Frank and thereby preserve his opportunity for continued legal appeal of his conviction, and in recognition of the State's failure to bring his killers to justice, and as an effort to heal old wounds, the State Board of Pardons and Paroles, in compliance with its Constitutional and statutory authority, hereby grants to Leo M. Frank a Pardon."

Frank's pardon did not clear him of Mary Phagan's murder, but in 2019, Fulton County District Attorney Paul Howard formed the Conviction Integrity Unit to reinvestigate past cases, including Leo Frank's case, and recommend whether any of the cases should be re-adjudicated. That decision is still pending.

A state marker commemorating the site of the lynching

Online Resources

Other books about 20th century history by Charles River Editors

Other books about Leo Frank on Amazon

Bibliography

Alphin, Elaine Marie. An Unspeakable Crime: The Prosecution and Persecution of Leo Frank. Carolrhoda Books, 2010.

Carter, Dan. "And the Dead Shall Rise: The Murder of Mary Phagan and the Lynching of Leo Frank". Journal of Southern History, Vol. 71, Issue 2 (May 2005), p. 491.

Dinnerstein, Leonard. The Leo Frank Case. University of Georgia Press, 1987.

Frey, Robert Seitz; Thompson-Frey, Nancy. The Silent and the Damned: The Murder of Mary Phagan and the Lynching of Leo Frank. New York, New York: Cooper Square Press (of Rowman & Littlefield), 2002.

Golden, Harry. A Little Girl is Dead. World Publishing Company, 1965. Retrieved June 25, 2011.

Lindemann, Albert S. The Jew Accused: Three Anti-Semitic Affairs (Dreyfus, Beilis, Frank), 1894–1915. Cambridge University Press, 1991.

Melnick, Jeffrey Paul. Black-Jewish Relations on Trial: Leo Frank and Jim Conley in the New South. University Press of Mississippi, 2000.

Oney, Steve. And the Dead Shall Rise: The Murder of Mary Phagan and the Lynching of Leo Frank. Pantheon Books, 2003.

Phagan Kean, Mary. The Murder of Little Mary Phagan. Horizon Press, 1987.

Samuels, Charles; Samuels, Louise Night Fell on Georgia, Dell, 1956

Free Books by Charles River Editors

We have brand new titles available for free most days of the week. To see which of our titles are currently free, click on this link.

Discounted Books by Charles River Editors

We have titles at a discount price of just 99 cents everyday. To see which of our titles are currently 99 cents, click on this link.

www.ingramcontent.com/pod-product-compliance
Lightning Source LLC
Chambersburg PA
CBHW080944120726
48003CB00011B/3293